Nature Writing Field Guide

For Teachers

Nature Writing Field Guide

For Teachers

Jan D. Wellik

San Diego, Calif.

To friends and family for your unconditional support, to the Wild Gift and the Peco Foundation in Sun Valley, Idaho for believing in the vision, and to the youth and teachers who open themselves to new discoveries –

With loving gratitude...

Contents

Educator Training

Professional Development Available

Educators at schools, nature centers and youth centers are invited to schedule a half-day or full-day Professional Development Training on-site or off-site. Contact the director for options: info@EcoExpressions.org

Learn how to adapt the Eco Expressions' Nature Writing Program to the specific needs of your classroom, school garden, or youth program.

Training includes hands-on, experiential professional development in utilizing the curriculum within this guidebook. Learn how to adapt the activities to students of all learning abilities in grades 1-12. Curriculum correlates with individual State and Federal Education Standards in Language Arts, Science, Visual Arts, and Physical Education.

Copyright Notice

How to use this book

This field guide is a tool to access and expand the literary creativity of your students. It serves as a unique curriculum to combine two major academic subjects, English and Science, into one scholastic adventure to revive the enthusiasm to learn.

The writing and art activities in this handbook can be used by a range of ages. The grade levels are merely a guideline based on average learning abilities for each grade. Please do not feel limited to select activities from a certain age group. All students have different capacities and interests, so try a variety, challenge your students to dig deeper, and you will be surprised by the wealth of creativity in your students.

Nature teaches us stillness.

Stillness is where creativity and solutions are born.

Practice stillness.

Program Overview

PURPOSE

Eco Expressions is a unique education program that emphasizes personal creativity and growth through outdoor exploration and writing. The nature writing curriculum in this guidebook offers young people a chance to explore the wonders of the natural world and expand literary and creative expression. Eco Expressions combines the healing powers of nature and writing to inspire positive change.

BENEFITS

Students benefit educationally, physically, psychologically and emotionally from the expressive arts utilized in this guidebook. The activities correlate with state and federal Education Standards, while also improving literacy and communication skills.

Suggested Activities for using this field guide

Outdoor activities:	Art activities:
Hiking	Drawing
Canoeing	Poetry
Plant Identification	Watercolor Pastels
Birdwatching	Photography
Wildlife Tracking	Creative Writing
Gardening	Mixed Media
Astronomy	Painting
Habitat Restoration	Journaling
Snowshoeing	Sculpture

METHOD

Elementary, middle, and high school students are empowered with the task of preservation through writing. Students observe and actively engage in the outdoors, while learning about the history of place. They develop a sense of community and record their observations. Creative and scientific writing are emphasized as a way to improve communication and social skills. Students learn how to establish individual viewpoints, respect others, and work together as educated, compassionate citizens.

Before, during, and after each outdoor activity, students are guided with observational and creative writing prompts to stimulate ecological, cultural and self-awareness.

Students keep a nature journal, taking field notes as they explore. Writing may reflect their discoveries in seeing the world from new perspectives and can be used as a life-long learning tool. The writing allows for freedom of expression and creativity. After each writing activity, students are encouraged to share with the group.

Students learn to identify botany and wildlife, and practice making comparisons in nature using metaphors and similes. By educating young people about the environment and providing them the tools for better decision-making in the future, we are helping to heal the ill-health of our ecosystems.

Personal experience in the outdoors instills a powerful level of respect and appreciation for others. This program goes a step further – We teach students how to use reflection tools like writing and drawing to observe the world around them, really experience it, and then discover their own place in the larger community.

Through sensory awareness, observation, and writing exercises, youth learn how to relate to the natural world, to feel at home in the outdoors. While exploring, students see the world from new perspectives. They develop patience, awareness, understanding, and improved communication skills. The same way that ecosystems need healthy intervention, many students in the classroom need a little extra help learning how to engage fully with the community in a positive way.

Behavioral Results

Anger Management	Relaxation
Stress Reducer	Decision-making
Problem Solving Skills	Listening Skills
Positive Thinking	Collaboration
Critical Thinking	Global Awareness
Self-Empowerment	Creativity
Enthusiasm	Sense of Belonging
Patience	Empathy

"Be a creature of the interior.

Don't look through it; look deeper and deeper." – Jill Robin Sisson

Writing Activities

Grades 1-5

Wilderness Warm-up:

- ❖ What is Nature?

- ❖ What does "Wilderness" mean to you?

- ❖ When have you experienced wilderness and what was it like?

Cloud Shapes:

Lie on the ground and watch the clouds go by overhead.

- ❖ What do you see in the cloud shapes? Animals, people, buildings?

- ❖ Draw a picture of what you see and describe it in a few sentences.

- ❖ Example: Gary Snyder's poem – *The Blue Sky:*

Sky. Horse with lightning feet, a mane like distant rain, the turquoise horse, a black star for an eye, white shell teeth.

Shadow Stories:

- ❖ Sitting under a tree, trace the sunlight that shines through the tree limbs onto your paper.

- ❖ What do the images create? Is there a story unfolding in the images? Listen carefully to your drawings, and let the light-shadows tell their stories.

- ❖ Looking at the shapes appearing on your paper. Write down words that come to mind, and tell a story about these shadow images.

Sensory Scavenger Hunt:

- ❖ Be ready to explore an area outdoors in an open area. Make hunt cards for each pair of students to find and observe one of the 4 sensory categories below. This is a scavenger hunt of the 5 senses, and students must draw and write what they find.

- ❖ Tell students NOT to pick or collect anything. They are observing the natural world without human interference. They are allowed to pick things up to look at them, but must put them back where they found them. For each of the senses below, students write a brief description of each discovery.

  - ❖ Find 5 different textures

  - ❖ Find 5 different shapes and draw them

  - ❖ Find 5 different smells

  - ❖ Find 5 different sounds

  - ❖ Bonus: What animal clues are nearby? (i.e.: tracks, half-eaten leaves, holes in trees, scat)

Geology Feels Like…

❖ Pass around different types of rocks and write about the textures they feel in their hands.

❖ Ask students to make comparisons of the rocks using similes and metaphors that relate to every items in their lives.

❖ Example: The surface of the volcanic rock feels like the rough bristles of the brush my parents use to clean the barbecue grill.

Nature's Perspective:

John Muir, a famous environmental writer, lowered himself down into icy glaciers and climbed to the top of great mountains, so that he could speak from the point of view of ice, rock, cloud and air.

❖ Lay on your belly. What do you see? Hear? Smell?

❖ Climb a hill. What do you see? Hear? Smell?

❖ Hang upside down or do a head stand. What do you see? Hear? Smell?

❖ Did you notice anything different from where you stood? How does perspective change what we see?

"We must somehow take a wider view, look at the whole landscape, really see it, and describe what's going on here." – Annie Dillard

Native American Names:

Historically, Native Americans gave each other names based on what they do outdoors or where they lived. Their names are often a story of their special skills. They named sites and special places they visited too.

- ❖ Make up names for each other based on what you like to do for fun outdoors, or where you live. What would your name be?

- ❖ <u>Example:</u> Deer Hunter sits, waiting, near Sound of Dripping Water beyond Frog Jump Rocks.

Bird Behavior:

Birdwatching involves learning how to identify the birds you see and hear, but it also means watching what they do, finding out how they find food, how they use their beaks to eat, how they react to their enemies, and where they build nests.

- ❖ Choose one bird to study, watch it move, where does it go, what does it do? Write down your observations.

- ❖ Act out bird behaviors you observe: strutting, scuffling, hopping, pecking, high knees, stalking, etc. and guess which birds might behave that way.

- ❖ <u>Example:</u> Bird Beaks

Acorn Woodpeckers hammer holes in tree trunks to store acorns. Hummingbirds have elongated, slender beaks to reach into long, narrow flowers to sip nectar.

Writing Activities

Grades 6-8

Zoom Out, Zoom In: Capturing a Snapshot of Nature

This activity helps students look with clear, observant eyes. Ask them to practice shutting out the rest of the world – friends talking, loud voices, growling stomachs. Start with the Zoom Out because it grounds participants in a specific space and time. Then Zoom In on the subject, for a close-up view.

This shifting between perspectives, like a camera, helps participants understand that there is more than one view, more than one right answer. It will help them to see multiple sides of an issue, and to understand perspectives beyond their own.

❖ **Zoom Out** – Stand in a spot with a good overview of the place around you. Observe 360-degrees as if you were a camera with a wide lens view. Get grounded in this place. For the next 3 minutes, use all of your senses to write a sensory inventory of what you observe about this landscape. This is an opening exercise, a chance to start off slowly. Allow students to choose their own style, it can be a descriptive list, a poem, etc.

Examples:

- prickly green grass
- rumbling tires on wooden bridge
- tired trees without leaves and bare branches

- wet pants from sitting on moist ground
- chirping and shrill bird calls
- light summery breeze
- stream rushing
- train horn sounds far in the distance
- canyon nestled against the hillside

"From 8,000 feet above sea level, a variety of habitats are visible in the Cuyamaca Mountains: desert, ocean, mountains and coastal sage scrub. The sun is at its peak point in the sky at noon and sweat is dripping off every hiker's forehead." – Jan D. Wellik

❖ **Zoom In** – Choose one aspect of the natural environment around you and focus on it. Trying to use only one of your senses, move closer to the object and describe the bird, squirrel, river sound, texture of tree bark, etc. in detail.

Examples:

Sunflower: "The sunflower leaned toward the dusty earth, as if bowing in prayer. Her slim yellow petals overlapped, encircling the brown of her core. Although hanging low, her stem stands strong and grows ever taller."

– Jan D.Wellik

Waves: "Listen to the surf and you will hear in it a world of sounds: hollow boomings and heavy roarings, great watery tumblings, long hissing seethes, sharp rifle-shot reports, splashes, whispers, the grinding undertone of stones…"   – Henry Beston

Squirrels: "The squirrel with mottled fur like a young doe is the look-out spotter. He jumped back in the hole not sure if it was safe when he spotted us. Then sat, body half way out, studying us. Another squirrel joined him. Sudden movement from humans sends the two running back into their underground tunnels. A few seconds later, the spotter reemerges, checking up on us. He seems to be saying, Yup, they're still there." – Jan D. Wellik

Lady Bug: "A lady bug dressed in a rusty shell with four black dots sits at the top of the wavering grass. Wind wobbles her foundation, the thin slice of grass that holds her up, but her reverie is not disturbed. She sits still, hanging sideways, not clinging, not clenching for dear life, just enjoying the wash of air over her, and slight touch of shade." – Jan D. Wellik

Animal Tracks:

❖ Follow a set of animal tracks and use a wildlife tracking guidebook to help you identify the type of animal you think it is.

❖ Write a fictional story of 3-5 paragraphs about what you imagine the animal is doing in this location and where you think it is going. Include other wildlife characters it may run into along the way.

A Place to Call Home:

❖ Walk around exploring animal homes, such as rock dens, hollow trees, ground burrows, ant hills, and bird nests.

❖ Write about these animal shelters. How do they differ? Why do the animals choose these places to make a home? What makes it a good place to live?

Adaptation to Environment:

A frog with moist skin that soaks up water from the damp rainforest would die within minutes in a hot, dry desert. However, a desert cactus grows slowly and conserves water by having thick stems and no leaves. It would be overshadowed by tropical trees and vines in a rainforest and cannot live without sunlight. Many animals and plants are well-suited to the environment where they live.

❖ Choose one animal here in this environment:

Write about how it survives in its natural habitat. What is it about this place that helps it live here? What would happen if it moved to another climate or habitat?

Team Tree Sketching:

- ❖ Choose a tree to study within eyesight. Ask all students to study the same tree for this activity.

- ❖ Each student sketches in their journal, the tree from the perspective of wherever they are standing or sitting. Sketch for about 3 minutes, and then ask them to stop, and pass their journal to the person on their right.

- ❖ Continue sketching the tree in the style of the person whose drawing you now hold in your hands. Imagine how this person would continue the sketch. Try not to project your own style onto their drawing. Draw for 3 minutes. Stop. Pass your journals to the person on the right again. Continue drawing in this new person's style for 3 minutes. Stop. Give journals back to original owners.

- ❖ Take a look at the drawing in your journal. Did the group stay consistent with your style?

- ❖ Does it look like a drawing you would have created? Discuss artistic style and how perspective changes the view of an image.

Writing Activities

Grades 9-12

Adventure Maps:

- ❖ Draw a map from memory about one of your favorite places outdoors that you explored as a child. (i.e.: backyard, river, tree fort, etc)

- ❖ Hike a trail and using a compass and measuring tape, record observations along the way to create a map of the route you took.

Life Bridges:

- ❖ Study a bridge and the body of water or land it crosses over. What impact has the bridge had on the environment? What is the history of this bridge? When was it created, and by whom?

- ❖ Now think metaphorically about bridges. Bridges connect gaps and make crucial crossings easier to pass. Write about a metaphorical bridge you've crossed over in life that linked one stage or experience to the next. What did you cross between? What was the experience that brought you over the bridge? What was the bridge made of?

Ecosystem Poem:

- ❖ Imagine that the place you call home includes the local ecosystem of all the living plants and animals that live in your neighborhood.

- ❖ Write a poem about your home from this new, all-encompassing sense of what makes up your community.

When I was Born:

- ❖ Write about the month in which you were born. Include the season, weather, stars, wildlife lifecycle stages, region of the country.

- ❖ Example: Read from *A Blizzard Year* by Gretel Ehrlich.

Nature Philosophy:

- ❖ What do you like about nature?

- ❖ What have you learned while being outdoors?

- ❖ What values has it shaped in your life?

- ❖ What would you like to teach adults about nature?

Bird Verbs:

❖ Pick a verb: hunting, eating, flying, grooming, socializing, communicating, diving, perching, hovering, landing, etc.

❖ Find a bird acting out this verb, then sit and silently observe for 5 minutes.

❖ Write about your action-packed observations.

❖ <u>Examples:</u>

Flying: "I caught only a glimpse of something like a bright torpedo that blasted the leaves where it flew." – Annie Dillard

Landing: "Carelessly, the birds land like D-Day soldiers on the beaches of Normandy. Packs of them, slamming into one another, elbowing and declaring their righteous territory with bomb-deafening shrieks. On the other side of the river is some of the best birdwatching in this country. Shorebirds rest here in between migrations. When they arrive, locals come running in all directions to witness their return." - Jan D. Wellik

Food Web:

"Where there are seeds and insects there will be birds and small mammals, and where these are will come the slinking, sharp-toothed kinds that prey on them." – Mary Austin

❖ Write about a food chain that exists in this habitat and how the species interconnect.

Lifecycles:

The lifecycle of insects is often much shorter, some only a matter of days, than the lifecycle of a mammal who can live 30 years in a healthy environment.

> ❖ Choose an insect or animal that exists in your ecosystem and write about its life cycle.
>
> ❖ Example: A caterpillar creates a chrysalis before turning into a butterfly.

Unusual Analogies:

- ❖ Make a list of clichés that you often hear people using to describe birds (i.e.: chirping, soaring high, free as a bird)

- ❖ Challenge yourself NOT to use these cliché analogies. Compare the sights and sounds of nature to unrelated things that most people would not think of easily.

- ❖ Examples:

"Far out at sea …near the horizon, is a pool of the loveliest blue I have ever seen here – a light blue, a petal blue, blue of the emperor's gown in a Chinese fairy tale." – Henry Beston

"The grass is like a woman dancing in a green dress."

– San Diego Girl Scout, age 8

History of a Raindrop:

John Muir traces the history of a raindrop in *My First Summer in the Sierras,*

"How interesting to trace the history of a single raindrop! ...Some go to the high snowy fountains to swell their well-saved stores; some into the lakes, washing the mountain windows, patting their smooth glassy levels, making dimples and bubbles and spray..."

❖ Write a wild thing's natural history – Where does it go? Where has it been? How does it impact the surrounding environment?

Human Impact:

❖ Write about the interrelationship between humans and nature in this environment that you are in right now.

❖ Examples:

"There are many areas in the desert where drinkable water lies within a few feet of the surface...Properly equipped it is possible to go safely across that ghastly sink, yet every year it takes its toll of death..."

- Mary Austin

Henry Beston writes about the triple wave tides along the Atlantic shore,

"Coast guard crews are all well aware of this triple rhythm and take advantage of the lull that follows the last wave to launch their boats."

Outdoor Character:

❖ Imagine someone you know who spends a lot of time outdoors – working, playing, studying. Write a physical description of that person as if s/he were a character in a story.

Example: John Muir wrote in *Great American Nature Writing*, p.134-135 about a shepherd's trousers.

Natural Forces:

❖ Choose a natural force that shapes this environment: snow, river, wind, sun, ice, or fire and describe how it changes the landscape based on the seasons, and over a span of years.

Wildfire:

❖ When was the last fire in your area?

❖ How did it affect the land and wildlife?

❖ Why is fire so important from an ecological standpoint?

Daily Assignment:

- ❖ Keep a notepad with you at all times – jot down nature discoveries and images that come to you during the day.

- ❖ Wake up! Open your eyes!

- ❖ Look high – Look low!

- ❖ Record your observations, and preservation will be rewarded in the stories you carry into history.

Group Poem:

This is a great wrap-up activity for all ages.

- ❖ At the end of a group hike bring everyone together and leave with a community memory about this shared space.

- ❖ Students contribute their favorite lines, or favorite lines that they heard someone else read, and a group poem is woven together with their words. It can be eloquent, simple, or silly – however it comes together…

Example:

Tiny feet, tiny toes, tiny head
bobs up and down,
spring push-ups.
Bird shadow crosses sunspot.
Ga-lump, ga-lump, another car over the bridge,
train whistle in the distance.
The water rushes,
ripples vibrate at the wind's small whispered suggestion.
Mmmm…the taste of carrot.

Spring Lesson Plan

Grades 6-8

(4 weeks – Each weekly lesson is 1 ½ hours.)

Week 1 – Tree Sketching

Word of the Week: Forestry

15 minutes: Get Centered –

Announce the word of the week and ask each student to say their name and the name of a tree that starts with the same letter as their name. Read a nature quote from the selection at the end of this field guide.

20 minutes: Journaling –

Students decorate the nature journals they will use for the next 4 weeks with images of nature from magazines and their own drawings.

25 minutes: Team Tree Sketching –

Go outdoors to do the Tree Sketching activity (page 19).

30 minutes: Neighborhood Tree Walk –

With a field guide to local trees, ask students to identify at least 3 trees in your neighborhood. Invite them to draw a sketch of a leaf from each of the trees in their journals. Compare to field guide illustrations.

Week 2 – Birdwatching

Word of the Week: Ornithology

15 minutes: Get Centered –

Announce the word of the week and welcome students back. Each person acts out a bird behavior as they say their name (i.e.: hopping, pecking, strutting, scuffling, high knees, stalking, flying). Choose student to read a nature quote aloud.

50 minutes: Birdwatching –

With binoculars and field guides, walk around the neighborhood near water or trees to observe birds and discuss bird behavior and spring migration. Compare to birds in field guides. Do Bird Verbs activity (page 22).

25 minutes: Journaling –

Ask students to start with the words, "Spring is a time when…."
Write for 5 minutes, then students share what they wrote with the group.

Week 3 – Adaptation

Word of the Week: Adaptation

15 minutes: Get Centered –

Announce the word of the week and ask each student to say one thing they like about their bedroom, or home where they live. Read a nature quote from selection.

30 minutes: Nature Hike –

Walk around the neighborhood studying human and animal homes. Discuss how animals choose where to live, i.e.: dens, hollow trees, ground burrows, nests. Draw a sketch of one of the homes you find.

20 minutes: Journaling –

❖ Pick one animal or plant here in this environment, and do Adaptation activity (page 18).

❖ Sketch a picture of its home and living environment.

Week 4 – Wildlife Tracking

Word of the Week: Riparian

10 minutes: Get Centered –

Describe the best time you ever had in a river, lake or ocean. Student reads a nature quote aloud.

90 minutes: Wildlife Tracking –

Bring journals to explore an area where tracks will be easily visible like a streambed, canyon or sandy surface. Just after a recent rain is a good time. Find wildlife tracks and identify with field guides.

- ❖ Pick a verb (i.e.: flying, hunting, eating, grooming, socializing, communicating, diving, perching, hovering, landing, etc) and match up wildlife with the verbs. Write about what you observe.

- ❖ Example: "I caught only a glimpse of something like a bright torpedo that blasted the leaves where it flew." – Annie Dillard

Winter Lesson Plan

Grades 6-8

(4 weeks – Each weekly lesson is 1 ½ hours.)

Week 1 – Sensory Scavenger Hunt and Mapmaking

Word of the Week: Respect

15 minutes: Get Centered -

Students introduce themselves and name one thing they liked about winter as a child. Leader reads a nature quote to the group.

20 minutes: Journaling –

Students decorate nature journals they will use for the next 4 weeks with magazine collage or draw images of nature and wildlife they enjoy.

30 minutes: Sensory Scavenger Hunt –

Discuss Sensory Observation. Divide into pairs, with each pair assigned one of the 5 senses and go outdoors for Sensory Scavenger Hunt (page 10).

30 minutes: Mapmaking –

Each pair will create a visual map on paper of the area they explored according to one of the sense. Then put them all together as one large map showing what the group observed using all 5 senses.

Week 2 – Mandalas and Meditation

Word of the Week: Meditation

10 minutes: Get Centered –

Name your favorite way to relax. Student reads a nature quote aloud.

10 minutes: Journaling –

Journal about one nice thing you have done for someone else this week.

30 minutes: Meditation –

Discuss meditation as a way to relax after a tough day at school or work. Practice getting quiet and focus on your center. Then try Movement Meditation – walking silently or yoga poses. (Warrior Pose is a great one for pre-teens and teens.) Ask them to experience the movement without talking for at least 5 minutes. Ask them to share what they felt after the experience.

45 minutes: Mandala Art –

Introduce the art of creating mandalas as a silent meditation and a way to manifest your hopes and dreams. Refer to mandala art books for ideas. Students will create their own mandalas for any positive force they would like, including: peace, happiness, success, love, good health, safety, etc. using pastels, paints or markers.

Week 3 – Snowflakes

Word of the Week: Water Cycle

10 minutes: Get Centered –

Students name a part of the Water Cycle and how it works. Student reads a nature quote.

40 minutes: Science Experiment –

Bring black paper and magnifying glass outside to catch falling snowflakes or sprinkle a few flakes from the ground onto paper. Quickly look with magnifying glass and identify in Ken Libbrecht's *Field Guide to Snowflakes*.

40 minutes: Journaling –

Draw the snowflakes they discovered and write a short story about where they would travel if they were a snowflake.

Week 4 – Mythology Stories

Word of the Week: Mythology

10 minutes: Get Centered –

Introduce the word of the week and talk about what mythology stories everyone knows. Student reads nature quote.

15 minutes: Mythology Chat –

Discuss mythological creatures or legends from around the world. (i.e.: Zeus, Lochness Monster, Medusa, Paul Bunyan, etc.)

30 minutes: Storytelling –

Take turns reading a mythological story aloud as a group, for example: *Earthmaker's Tales: North American Indian Stories about Earth Happenings* by Gretchen Will Mayo. (The earthquake fable is a great example to use.)

30 minutes: Story Writing –

❖ Students write their own fictional mythology: a short-story based on an element of the natural world. Encourage creative storytelling.

❖ Students could pick from the following natural forces: blizzard, avalanche, hurricane, rainbow, lightning, hot springs, tornado, typhoon, etc. They must include main components of a story: who is causing the action, why they are doing this, where it happens and when it might occur.

OR

60 minutes: Sculptures –

❖ Build a snow or sand sculpture of a mythological creature as a group.

OR

❖ Build a sculpture with clay as a group, or individually, of a creature from a mythological legend discussed.

Garden Art Lesson Plan

Grades 1-5

(6 weeks – Each weekly lesson is 1 ½ hours.)

Week 1

Word of the Day: Organic

Garden Map –

❖ Talk as a group about where each plant will go. Students draw a garden map in their journals of what the garden will look like.

Planting –

❖ Students plant herbs, vegetable seedlings, or seeds, depending on age of students, length of program and long-term plan for the garden. Examples: mint, lemongrass, chamomile, and lavender.

❖ Compare smells and uses of the herbs. Discuss what makes a garden organic and healthy.

Journaling –

❖ Decorate garden journals with magazine pictures and drawings.

❖ Discuss Garden Observers' role each week at the beginning of lesson. Starting next week, two students will observe the garden each week, measuring plants and record growth in their journals along with weather, temperature, and overall health of the garden.

Week 2

Word of the Day: Geology

Journaling –

   ❖ Garden Observers

Rock Hunt –

   ❖ Go on a Rock Hunt and let each student select one rock to bring back to the garden. Bring magnifying glasses to talk about geology of the rocks.

Painting –

   ❖ Paint rocks with inspirational words about what they like about gardening: *Beauty. Joy. Wonder. Love Grows Here. Miracles.*

   ❖ Place the painted rocks in the garden for inspiration.

Week 3

Word of the Day: Botanical

Journaling –

❖ Garden Observers

Nature Hike –

❖ As a group, take a short nature hike to collect fallen leaves and flowers. Try to identify plants and flowers using field guides.

❖ Place collected leaves and flowers in a flower press for next week's art project.

Week 4

Word of the Day: Lifecycle

Journaling –

❖ Garden Observers

Flower Placemats –

❖ Make pressed flower placements by gluing dried flowers and leaves to cardstock or construction paper. Laminate with clear, sticky vinyl paper to hold the flowers on the paper.

❖ Discuss the lifecycles of flowers and plants used in the art project.

Week 5

Word of the Day: Plumage

Journaling –

❖ Garden Observers

Birdwatching –

❖ Go birdwatching with binoculars to identify and describe bird calls and observations.

❖ Learn about the differences between bodies, beaks and feet of the birds and how they use them to live and eat.

Wild Bird Game –

❖ Each student starts with a blank sheet of construction paper folded in thirds. Ask them to draw a bird's head with beak on the top 1/3 of the sheet. They can draw any kind of bird they choose.

❖ Fold the top over so it can't be seen, and pass it to the person on the right.

❖ Add a bird's body with wings to the 2nd fold of the paper. Make sure they don't look at the top part that is folded over.

❖ Fold over the paper again, so that the top 2 drawings are hidden.

❖ Pass the paper to the person on the right again, and that person adds the bird's feet to the bottom 3rd of the page.

❖ Pass back to the first person and open it up to see your Wild Bird!

Week 6

Word of the Day: Horticulture

Garden Party –

- ❖ Time to celebrate the harvest!

- ❖ Make teas using herbs from the garden and use the flower art placemats they made.

- ❖ Sketch the garden they helped to create, with pastels, paints, or colored pencils. Look back at journals and ask them to name one new thing they learned in the past 6 weeks.

Nature Quotes and Poetry

"The land holds a collective memory…

Perhaps our only obligation is to listen and remember."

- Terry Tempest Williams

The beauty of the trees,

the softness of the air,

the fragrance of the grass,

speaks to me.

The summit of the mountain,

the thunder of the sky,

the rhythm of the sea,

speaks to me…

And my heart soars.

- Chief Dan George

I'm the mad cosmic

Stones plants mountains

Greet me bee rats

Lions and eagles

Stars twilights dawns

Rivers and jungles all ask me

What's new How you doing?

And while stars and waves have something to say

It's through my mouth they'll say it

-Vicente Huidobro

We do not weave the web of life,

We are merely a strand in it.

Whatever we do to the web,

we do to ourselves.

-Chief Seattle

Every time you breathe in, thank a tree.

- John Wright

When the animals come to us,

asking for our help,

will we know what they are saying?

When the plants speak to us,

in their delicate, beautiful language,

will we be able to answer them?

When the planet herself

sings to us in our dreams,

will we be able to wake ourselves, and act?

- Gary Lawless

My words are tied in one

With the great mountains,

With the great rocks,

With the great trees,

In one with my body

And my heart.

- Yokuts Indian prayer

"If you can learn to immerse yourself in the ordinary things that are very close by, you start to understand what it means to exist in nature. By establishing a relationship with nature based on particulars, you begin to break the habit of generalizing about nature from a distance. This is the first step toward changing our approach to the land – and that starts with seeing."   – Judith Belzer, painter

A good way to start thinking about nature,

talk about it.

Rather talk to it,

talk to the rivers, to the lakes,

to the winds, as to our relatives.

- John Lame Deer

Give us the strength to understand,

and the eyes to see.

Teach us to walk the soft earth as relatives to all that live.

- Sioux prayer

For everything that is taken, something has to be given in return.

If you merely take in a breath and stop there, you will die.

Life is not giving or taking, it is give and take.

- Elizabeth Roberts

We give-away our thanks to the earth

which gives us our home.

We give-away our thanks to the rivers and lakes

which give-away their water.

We give-away our thanks to the trees

which give-away fruit and nuts.

We give-away our thanks to the wind

which brings rain to water the plants.

We give-away our thanks to the sun

who gives-away warmth and light.

All beings on earth: the trees, the animals, the wind and the rivers,

give-away to one another

so all is in balance.

We give-away our promise to begin to learn

how to stay in balance with all the earth.

- Dolores La Chapelle

As I set forth into the day

the birds sing with new voices

and I listen with new ears

and give thanks.

You can see forever

when the vision is clear

in this moment

each moment

I give thanks.

- Harriet Kofalk

Step out into the Planet.

Draw a circle a hundred feet round.

Inside the circle

are 300 things nobody understands, and, maybe

nobody's ever really seen.

How many can you find?

- Lew Welch

Praise wet snow falling early

Praise the invisible sun burning

beyond the white cold sky,

giving us light.

Praise flow and change, night

and the pulse of day.

- Denise Levertov

Look deeply: I arrive in every second

to be a bud on a spring branch,

to be a tiny bird, with wings still fragile,

learning to sing in my new nest,

to be a caterpillar in the heart of a flower,

to be a jewel hiding itself in a stone...

Please call me by my true names,

so I can wake up,

and so the door of my heart can be left open,

the door of compassion.

-Thich Nhat Hanh

Clouds are flowing in the river, waves are flying in the sky.

Life is laughing in a pebble. Does a pebble ever die?

Flowers grow out of the garbage, such a miracle to see.

What seems dead and what seems dying makes for butterflies

to be.

Life is laughing in a pebble, flowers bathe in morning dew.

Dust is dancing in my footsteps and I wonder who is who.

Clouds are flowing in the river, clouds are drifting in my tea,

On a never-ending journey, what a miracle to be!

- Eveline Beumkes

Water flows over these hands

May I use them skillfully

to preserve our precious planet.

- Thich Nhat Hanh

Printed in the United States
221115BV00002B/34/P